Minimalism

A guide to improving your

life with minimalism

Anthony Hill

Table of Contents

Introduction

Doing more with less. Keeping things simple. Living intentionally. These are just some of the phrases you may have heard about minimalism. Or maybe you haven't heard anything about minimalism but are curious and want to learn more. Whether you know a little, a lot, or nothing about minimalism, you've come to the right place!

Minimalism has risen in popularity in recent years as more people want to simplify their lives. Some reasons for this include being more organized and having to think less about their stuff, saving money for an early retirement, or doing their part in reducing consumption for environmental reasons. But more on that later.

What You'll Learn

Life is busy and time is precious. Sometimes it seems like we have a million and one things to do. We have so many decisions to make during the day. We have to decide what to wear, what and when to eat, what we should do with our free time, who we should spend time with, and when we should clean our homes. And that's not to mention getting ourselves to work and making decisions all day on the job. It can be overwhelming and stressful. But maybe there's a different way to live—and maybe it's a simpler way.

In this book you'll learn what minimalism is. You'll discover the basic principles and the benefits of minimalism. You'll also learn how to get started on your minimalism journey, including how to get rid of your unnecessary possessions. If you're worried that you'll have to do away with your tropical houseplant, shoes, or record collections, fear not! You'll learn to figure out what is essential to you and how to be more intentional as you move into a more minimalist lifestyle.

Starting on a minimalist journey isn't always easy. There are challenges when learning about and adopting a new lifestyle. This book will give you the tools and inspiration to decide what's important to you. One person's minimalist journey can look entirely different from another's. As you're reading through this book, try to apply what you read to your own lifestyle. It's important to be honest with yourself about where you are now and where you want to be.

You'll also read about the minimalist movement and how it relates to the FIRE (Financial Independence, Retire Early) movement. If you've dreamed about being more financially independent so you can have more freedom, minimalism might help you get there! After all, it costs money to buy and maintain things.

Having too much stuff can make life stressful. Maintaining, storing, and using your possessions uses a lot of brain power that can be put towards other things. But there is another way to live—a way that allows you to have more time in the mornings because you're not deciding between eight different outfits and six different breakfast choices. It's a way that teaches you to say no to things that don't matter, because you've realized what does. There is a better way—minimalism.

Chapter 1: Minimalism: What It Is and the Basic Principles

The Concept of Minimalism

Let's start with what minimalism is not. It is not a fad. It does not mean you have to get rid of all your possessions, or that you must live alone in one room with no furnishings, one set of dishes, and one set of clothes.

Minimalism is a way of simplifying your life. It means eliminating what you do not use or need. It provides you the time and space to figure out what is important to you so you can start living intentionally—whatever that means for you. Whether you want to focus on your health, have more time for family, hobbies, learning a new skill, or you simply want to declutter your home, minimalism frees you from excess, so you have more time and energy to focus on what's important.

"Excess what?" You might ask. Excess anything. It could be your excess possessions, excess social obligations, being in debt, or having too many distractions. Minimalism helps you examine your life to figure out what is meaningful to you. So, if your collection of bobbleheads is meaningful to you and brings you joy, then don't worry! You don't have to part with it!

Minimalism frees you from that feeling of having to buy things in order to be happy and satisfied. Constantly striving to have new furniture, technology, clothing, or vehicles, and continually planning outings and vacations can be exhausting. Minimalism helps you to rid yourself of what you deem unnecessary but allows you to keep the stuff you want and do the things you truly want to do—whatever you decide adds value to your life.

The Basic Principles

Although there are no one-size-fits-all rules for minimalism, there are some basic principles. Consider these guidelines as you navigate your way to a more minimalist lifestyle.

Figure out what's important to you and get rid of anything outside of that. What are your priorities? What is essential to you? Do you want more time in the morning to spend with your kids, or to journal and do yoga? If getting dressed in the morning takes up more time than you'd like to admit, maybe it's time to figure out the pieces in your wardrobe that make you look and feel best and give away the rest.

Minimalism doesn't just encompass the physical items you own, although that is a large component of this lifestyle. Minimalism also encourages you to be intentional about how you spend your time each day. Most of us complain that there aren't enough hours in the day, yet we waste countless hours on things that for many of us don't add any value to our lives. For you, perhaps this is time spent mindlessly browsing social media, watching TV, or online shopping for things you don't really need.

Whether your priority is family, friends, your health, work, or your hobbies, you need to identify what makes you happy and what's getting in the way of being happy. Then look at getting rid of what is getting in the way. It may be working too much overtime so you can't hang out with your friends, spending time with people who don't make you feel good instead of the two or three people you can be yourself with, or spending too much time zoning out on the computer instead of working on your passion project.

Figuring out what is important to you is the cornerstone to a happy life. You can go through life on autopilot, not doing any of the things you really want to do and not realizing how much time has passed until it's too late. Or you can determine what makes you happy, identify what gets in the way of that happiness, and get rid of those things! That's minimalism in a nutshell.

Be intentional with everything, but especially with your spending. Being a minimalist doesn't mean you can't have things. It simply means that you put more thought into what you're buying, instead of buying things spur-of-the-moment. Just because you walk by your local store that is advertising two T-shirts for $15 doesn't mean you need to run in and buy them if you've already got a similar T-shirt or two.

The idea behind minimalism is to live intentionally. It's not about depriving yourself. It's about not giving into consumerism that tells us to buy, buy, buy. If you see something that you love and you know you'll use, by all means you should buy it. But if you're robotically buying things because you feel it's what you need to do, take a pause and examine why you feel that way.

Again, you make your own rules. Minimalism is about not buying things you don't need. If you think you need five identical yellow T-shirts, go for it! The important thing is that you feel comfortable with why you have five identical yellow T-shirts.

Which brings us to…

Quality over quantity and functional beauty are important concepts. Let's face it: those two T-shirts for $15 are probably made from cheap material and will fall apart in less than a year. As mentioned earlier, there are no hard and fast rules, but many minimalists, because they are being intentional about their purchases, favor quality over quantity. One well-made T-shirt (within your budget, of course) lasts longer, looks better, and takes up less space than two cheap t-shirts. It's also better for the environment, but more on that later. If you find the thought of spending too much money up front scary, think about the cost per wear. Cost per wear is the idea that the value of an item is related to how many times you wear it.

Functional beauty is the idea that something that can be beautiful and useful at the same time. Think about filling your home with stunningly beautiful but absolutely uncomfortable furniture; you wouldn't want to use it. But make that furniture both beautiful and comfortable and you have a winning combination. Having beautiful, comfortable furniture means you don't need to have the "good" room with the nice, uncomfortable furniture for when guests visit and the "everyday" room with your comfy chair. It means you can be comfortable all the time and enjoy how your furniture looks!

Replace or repair. Don't upgrade. Unless you upgrade with intention. Being a minimalist doesn't mean you have to live in sparse surroundings. It means you think about what you need and what will add value to your life. If your five-year-old winter boots are timeless but they have worn-out heels, your nearest cobbler can repair them for you, and you can keep on wearing them if they're comfortable and make you feel good.

Being intentional means you don't look at your worn-out heels and automatically think "time for a new pair of boots." Living a minimalist lifestyle teaches you to control that impulse to automatically replace or upgrade.

Maybe you have a television that works perfectly fine and meets all of your needs, but your neighbors just bought a new television that looks amazing. You see that the store down the street is having a massive sale. Why not treat yourself? Well, being a minimalist doesn't mean you shouldn't treat yourself. But it means putting some thought into why you want that shiny new television. Is it because you're a homebody who spends their time watching television and movies? If that is what makes you happy, if it's how you want to spend your time, and you think the new television will add value to your life, by all means you should buy it and rehome your old television. But if you want to buy a new television simply to compete with your neighbors or because you feel you should have the latest technology, it's probably a good time to examine your intentions.

Try to place less value on material possessions. We all have an item or two that is sentimental to us. It could be a vase from your grandmother or a mug from your great-aunt Gertrude. The important thing to keep in mind is that things are temporary so they can only bring you temporary joy. Attachment to things can be devastating if the thing we love so much breaks. It's our relationships and experiences that bring us true joy. You'll remember the belly laugh you had with a friend more than you will remember something they gave to you.

Of course, if your grandmother's vase brings you joy, by all means keep it and make sure you display it. But if you're keeping it out of guilt or because your mother says you should, it might be time to part with it.

Minimalism doesn't just apply to your physical possessions. Removing the excess also applies to things like your time commitments, your relationships, your hobbies, your goals, and your diet.

Here comes that I-word again: *intention*. If you spend 25 hours a week outside of your full-time job volunteering for different organizations because you feel you have to, it's time to be honest with yourself. Are you volunteering at those different places because you feel it makes you look like a better person? Volunteering is a noble pursuit, but would you rather spend more time volunteering at one or two organizations that align with your values instead of spreading yourself thin at five organizations? Or do you truly enjoy spending your time that way? Think about quality over quantity—what adds value to your life and what speaks to your heart. Choose to not spread yourself too thin.

Are you living to work or working to live? If you're working more than you'd like, perhaps it's time to consider working smarter and not harder or longer. Minimalism means trimming the excess and streamlining. Consider this the next time you say yes to a meeting you may not need to attend or volunteering for a task that will keep you working overtime and away from something else you would rather be doing.

The same can be said for relationships. Are you spending time with people who make you happy or do you feel yourself wishing you were somewhere else when you're with certain people? Examining the reasons why you hold on to certain relationships will help you realize what relationships are important to you and which ones are just excess. There are all sorts of reasons we choose to spend time with people we don't necessarily jive with. Figure out those reasons. Looking at the relationships where you feel like you can be yourself without judgement will help you determine who you want to spend more time with.

Being intentional with your eating can also be part of being a minimalist. If you find yourself mindlessly snacking any time of the day despite not being hungry, you may want to think about why you're doing that. Are you bored? Lonely? Sad?

Being intentional about your diet doesn't mean you can't eat delicious food or be flexible about what you eat. Minimalism is about keeping it simple and removing the excess. It's about simplifying the time you spend shopping, cooking, and cleaning.

Reevaluate on a regular basis. This means looking at your possessions, relationships, commitments, and diet regularly to see if any excess needs to be trimmed. Priorities change over time, and what once brought you joy may now be a chore. Ask yourself if anything has become a burden or stopped you from seeing people or doing the things that you consider essential. If so, it's time to let whatever it is go.

Appreciate what you have. Because minimalism is about being mindful and intentional about buying new things, it helps you appreciate what you have. This creates a beautiful cycle of buying less and appreciating what you have more, which in turn makes you want to buy less! Having less means appreciating what we do have. It also makes us realize that we don't need a lot of things to lead a meaningful life.

Be you. The lovely thing about minimalism is you decide how you want to live. You decide what's important to you and what you value. When you choose what makes you happy and what adds value to your life, you grow as a person. You decide for yourself who you want to be, who you want to spend time with, what you want to do, and where you want to go. Doesn't that sound like freedom? Because that's what minimalism is—freedom to choose for yourself and not be bound by society or other people's expectations.

A Closing Note on the Principles

Minimalism is all about simplicity. Simplifying your time, your personal relationships, your things, and your goals. Minimalism isn't about being selfish – it's about being intentional. If you pare down to only the things, people, and commitments that make you happy and add value to your life, not only will you be happier, but the people you choose to spend time with will be getting the best version of you!

Chapter 2: Reap What You Sow: The Benefits of Minimalism

Now that you've read some basic principles, let's look at some benefits of minimalism, of which there are many.

What You'll Get Out of Minimalism

You can get so much out of minimalism. The first and foremost benefit, as mentioned earlier, is freedom. You'll have the freedom to be yourself, to make your own choices, to live an authentic life, and to not obsess over owning the latest gadget. For many, this results in freedom from stress, and can even set you on the path to financial freedom.

Time

Have you thought about how much time it takes to clean, maintain, and store your stuff? It is a fact that when you own less, you spend less time on the care and maintenance of said stuff. And when you only buy the things that you need, you will spend less time shopping for more stuff. Having fewer possessions also makes it easier to keep a tidier home, as you spend less time cleaning and organizing.

Spending less time shopping for things, transporting them home, and maintaining them means you will have more time to do the things that you want to do. It means you can take that painting course you have been thinking about, spend more quality time with friends, exercise, write a book, or do whatever it is that you feel the urge to pursue.

You will also be able to find things more quickly. If you have ever looked through an unorganized drawer filled with mismatched plastic containers, you will understand! Paring down that drawer to include only the containers you need will save you loads of time when you are trying to put away any leftovers.

Having less clothing makes it much easier to get ready in the morning, or at any time really. Many minimalists have a uniform of sorts that they wear as their signature look. Having a small selection of clothes that you love means you can go to your closet, choose the items in your uniform, put them on, and be ready for your day. There are no decisions to be made so you are not starting your day standing in front of your closet thinking, "What am I going to wear today?" Having a uniform doesn't have to be boring. You get to choose your signature look, whatever that may be.

Perspective

Having less and realizing you need less can provide you with a new perspective. After a few months of living with less, you may find you will look around in contentment and wonder how you lived with a bunch of unnecessary things in the first place.

Being happier with less means that your relationship with money may change. Like most people in the western world, you likely grew up wanting to have a lot of money. After living a minimalist lifestyle for a little while, you will notice that your desire to buy more is dwindling. This may lead you to realize you no longer need to pursue money the way you used to.

Minimalism may even give you a different perspective on what it means to be successful. Once you have lived as a minimalist for a little while and find that you are happier with less, your definition of success may change.

Patience

Minimalism helps you develop patience; it takes patience to gradually pare down your belongings. You will also learn to enjoy the journey of life and not the immediate but short-lived satisfaction that comes from buying things.

Focus

Living with less means you can focus on what is important to you. This could look like having less clutter in the house so you can focus on learning an instrument in your home because you have more space. Or it may look like stopping some of the time-wasting activities you engage with so that you can focus on taking a course or spending more time with friends and family.

Community

Minimalism can lead to a new community. There is a rapidly growing group of people in the world who practice minimalism in its many forms. There are a variety of Facebook groups, YouTube channels, and internet forums dedicated to this lifestyle where you can connect with like-minded people on a similar path.

Self-Awareness

Minimalism makes you look at yourself and ask what you want out of life. You need to ask yourself why you are holding on to certain possessions and relationships and if you really need them in your life. It also makes you look at how you currently spend your time in comparison to how you would ideally like to spend it.

All of these questions lead to more self-awareness. It is important to examine your life and ask yourself what is important to you. Only then can you begin to live an intentional life.

Energy

Taking care of all your stuff takes a lot of energy, and so does pretending to be happy in any relationship that no longer serves you. And if you have committed to spending your time in ways that do not make you happy, that will suck your energy too. Trimming any excessive stuff, people, or commitments means you will have more energy to do the things you want to do, including spending time with people who make you happy.

More space

You may live in a small apartment or a big house. But once you begin your minimalist journey, you'll find you have more space no matter where you live because you get choosy about how much stuff you want and need. You buy less which means you have less possessions taking up room in your home. And once you have more space, you'll find you want to buy even less because you like the feeling of space. It's a lovely chain of events!

Having Less Stuff Makes It Easier to Travel

When you've got a large collection of clothing, it can be difficult to pack for a trip. If you're someone who travels frequently for work or for leisure, you'll know that packing lightly can make your travels a lot more enjoyable!

Fun

Minimalism puts a spotlight on experiences over stuff. The experiences can be free, or you can use the money you save on buying less stuff to pay for an experience. Once you start experiencing more and buying less, you will likely find that you are having more fun!

More Visual Satisfaction

If you've never heard of this, it simply means that you like what you see. Having an uncluttered, neat and tidy home is refreshing!

Creativity

You might be wondering what being a minimalist and creativity have to do with each other. Well, lots actually! When you start examining your life and what excess you need to rid yourself of, you are free to get creative with how you want your life to look. In addition, having less clutter to distract you and more free time available each day provides you with the opportunity to follow any creative pursuits you desire!

Your Relationships with Other People

Evaluating your relationships and only spending time with the people who you can be yourself around means you'll be focusing on relationships that hold real substance. Spending quality time in these relationships will only serve to make them even better.

Being an Individual

Being a minimalist means not following the latest trends. You are free to choose who you want to be and how you want to live. You focus on what adds value to your life and what is important to you. Everything else is superfluous.

Let's Talk About Your Health in Minimalism

Mental Health

As mentioned earlier, minimalism can make you appreciate what you have, and being grateful can lead to better mental health. Some of the benefits of being grateful include being more optimistic, improving your mood, and feeling more connected to people in your life. When the world is screaming out, "More! More! More!" be a rebel and be grateful for what you have instead of going out and blindly consuming.

A cluttered home can make some people anxious and stressed. Sometimes just looking at all of your stuff and contemplating what you need to do with it can be stressful. Long-term stress is associated with things like digestive problems, memory loss, premature aging, weight gain, sleep issues, and chronic fatigue.

Having a clutter-free environment encourages a sense of calm. Your home is your sanctuary—it's the place you start your day and the place you come to after being out in the world. It is your refuge. It should be welcoming so when you wake up or step through your door at the end of the day, you feel relaxed. If the clutter in your home is making you stressed, it's time to make a change.

Scaling back on unnecessary actions and commitments leads to more time to do what you want and need to do. Consider the things you do that waste time and what you could be doing instead. If you're robotically watching YouTube videos because you don't want to be alone with yourself and your thoughts, you might consider a solitary activity that relieves stress. That could be reading, meditating, or coloring. Think about what it would look like to cut back on the things you do that waste time and what you could do instead.

Physical Health

Since minimalism helps you be more intentional with your eating, you can start to look at the things you consume that aren't healthy. If you start buying less packaged and processed foods and begin to eat cleaner, you'll reap the physical health benefits.

Eating more whole foods and less chemical-laden foods full of salt and sugar can reduce your risk of high blood-pressure, stroke, type-2 diabetes, and heart disease.

With the extra time you have from owning less stuff and having fewer obligations, you'll discover you have more time for exercise. It doesn't have to be a two-hour sweat session at the gym. It could be a 20-minute walk with a friend around your neighborhood. Or you could take that yoga class you've been thinking about. We all know the benefits of exercise, including better sleep, weight loss, and lower blood pressure.

Speaking of better sleep, having more time means you can get into a nightly bedtime routine that might help you sleep better. Sleep is important for both your physical and mental health. Having a consistent bedtime routine can dramatically improve your sleep quality.

Finally, one not so obvious health benefit from minimalism is that owning less stuff means there is less dust in your home. That means less dust mites and less allergens which makes it easier for you to breathe.

Minimalism and Your Finances

This may be stating the obvious but if you're only buying what you need and what adds value to your life, you're probably buying less than you did before. Let's face it: stuff is expensive. Buying less than before means that you can start saving money. Living a more simplistic lifestyle usually means spending less because you're consuming less.

As mentioned earlier, minimalism is about trimming the excess. It means looking at what adds value to your life. When you start on your road to minimalism, you need to look at your lifestyle and figure out what is necessary and what you can get rid of. This means being brutally honest with yourself about things like your self-care, hobbies, possessions, and how often you go out for dinner, to the movies, or out for drinks. Are you staying within your budget, or are you mindlessly spending money on the latest gadgets?

Becoming a minimalist means asking questions like the ones above and also asking questions before you make a purchase. When looking at something that you are thinking of buying, you could ask yourself if you have something similar at home that fulfills the same purpose and if what you are looking at is the best use of your money. Try to think of how many hours you had to work to make the money to pay for the item. You are trading your precious time for whatever it is—it better be worth it!

Environmental Benefits

Buying less means having less to throw out. And it's not just the things themselves; it's the myriad of packaging that consumer items come with nowadays.

Since minimalism is about buying less but better stuff, it means the things you buy will last longer. That means that less ends up in landfill.

The fast fashion industry—fashion that is cheaply made in large quantities—uses many natural resources. According to Business Insider, the fashion industry releases more carbon than international flights and maritime shipping combined (McFall-Johnsen, 2019). The fashion industry is the second largest consumer of water, needing about 700 gallons to produce one cotton shirt and about 2,000 gallons to produce one pair of jeans (Maiti, 2020).

Sobering, isn't it? Being intentional about what you buy and choosing quality over quantity will help ensure you aren't contributing to the world of fast fashion and its detrimental impacts on the environment.

Living within your means and not living in a home that is too big for you can be good for the environment. You don't have to heat and cool a big space, and you don't have to buy cleaning products to clean a big space.

When you are intentional with your eating and only buy food that nourishes your body, you're helping the environment. So often, we buy food because we're tempted by the packaging (which ends up in the landfill) and the marketing of the product. Many of us buy too much food and much of it goes to waste.

Chapter 3: How to Get Started

If you've made it this far, it's likely that you want to try your hand at minimalism, but where to start? In this chapter, we'll discuss the different ways you can begin to adopt a minimalist lifestyle.

How to Start

First, think about the reasons you want to try minimalism, and be honest with yourself. For many of us, getting rid of our possessions can be challenging, even if they're possessions we rarely, if ever, use. Being clear about your reasons for embracing minimalism will provide the much-needed encouragement to give this lifestyle a proper go!

You may want to write down why you want to try minimalism. That way, in a few weeks or months if you are struggling with getting rid of some of your stuff, paring down your schedule or wanting to shop all of the sales, you can remind yourself why you started this journey in the first place. Think about some of the rules you want to implement. For instance, do you want to live with just one of each thing you have? Or will you allow yourself more than one of certain possessions? Do you simply want to declutter your home, or do you want to use minimalism in more areas of your life, like your relationships, your finances, your diet, and your activities? Will you hold on to possessions for sentimental reasons or can you get rid of them and hold on to the memories instead?

Getting Rid of Your Unnecessary Stuff

You may feel overwhelmed when you look around at all of your possessions, but this doesn't have to be a daunting task! Here are a few steps to simplify the process of removing the unnecessary from your life.

Look for Duplicates

The first thing you can do is go through your things and look for any duplicates or triplicates. Hopefully you don't have any quadruplicates of things that are not part of a collection, but you can look for those too! Use a box or a bag to store any duplicates. Things you might have duplicates of, but don't necessarily need duplicates of, include kitchen utensils, pens or pencils, post-it notes, beach towels, scissors, rubber bands, mugs, cutting boards, games, puzzles, or sports equipment. You might be shocked to see just how much space is being needlessly taken up by duplicates.

As you go through your items, ask yourself why you need more than one or two of each thing. You might also want to consider if you love each thing, if it is useful, and if it makes you happy when you look at it. Be honest—are you keeping something out of guilt because you spent too much money on it or because someone gave it to you? If you spent too much money on an item that you don't use, you have already paid for it. Stop paying for it now with stress and guilt and get rid of it!

Once you have gone through your home and put the duplicates in a box or bag, label it "duplicates." Then put it in a closet or somewhere you can't see it. Put a reminder in your calendar for two months from the day you store your duplicates box or bag. If you don't miss or have not used those items in two months, donate them. Keeping them in your home for a couple of months takes some of the stress away. You still have the items so you know if you start missing one or two of them, you can pull them from the bag and start using them again. But if, after two months, you haven't thought about them at all, you ought to remove them from your home.

Of course, if you feel that you want or need to keep a duplicate of something because you'll use it, by all means you should keep it. If you feel strongly about a certain duplicate possession and don't want it to be part of the exercise, try just putting it in a drawer or out of your sight for a couple of weeks. After that time has passed, ask yourself if you've missed the item or if you really need it "just in case."

Go Clutter-Free

Another thing that you can try when starting on your minimalist journey is to create a clutter-free zone. This could be anywhere you want to try having less clutter: your bedside table, your dining room table, the top of your fridge, or a countertop. Remove what you think of as the clutter from that area. Start small. If you like what you see, you will want to create other clutter-free areas that will eventually grow throughout your home. The trick is to use baby steps.

When you have enough energy and are ready to tackle your junk drawer, pull the drawer completely out. You want to make sure there is nothing stuck behind it. Pull everything out of the drawer and take an inventory. Are there any expired coupons, old grocery store lists, or anything broken? If so, discard those right away. If you find duplicates, you can add those to your duplicates box or bag. Once you have discarded the garbage and stored the duplicates, put the remaining things in an organizer of some sort. This way your junk drawer will look better, and you will be less tempted to make it a catch-all. Your junk drawer is definitely a place you will want to revisit on a regular basis to make sure you are not adding to it.

Tackling Your Wardrobe

Okay, this can be a big one for some people—your wardrobe. Having a cluttered wardrobe can be a huge time suck. It also means you need the space to store all of your clothes. And if you have a lot of seasonal clothes that don't fit into your closet, you need to find a spot to store those too. Once again, start small. This doesn't have to be scary and you do not have to rid yourself of all your clothes. Remember that minimalism is not about depriving yourself.

The first step is to take an inventory of all your clothes. This is where you once again have to be very honest with yourself. Think about how often you wear each item, whether each piece compliments what you have, if each item fits you properly, what items need to be repaired, and finally, if the piece of clothing makes you feel good when you put it on. If you come across something and wonder why you haven't worn it in a long time, try wearing it out of your house. You will quickly be reminded why you haven't worn it. It could just be that it was hiding behind all of your other clothes and you forgot about it. Or maybe it's not a great fit for you but it looked good in the store.

Something important to keep in mind when going through your clothing is if it fits your current lifestyle. Perhaps you bought a beautiful, but totally impractical pair of shoes that were on sale.

Be honest with yourself about how often you will wear those shoes, if at all. This is not to say you should get rid of the shoes if you absolutely love them, but there are alternatives to keeping them. If you do have a fancy party to attend in the future, you could always borrow a pair of nice shoes from a friend or family member, and there are many places now popping up that rent out formal wear. The idea is to think of how many times you wear an item and how much space it takes up in your home and in your life.

Again, if you are holding on to items because you spent a lot of money on them, that is not a reason to keep them. The guilt you feel for the money you spent will not bring that money back. Holding on to the items makes you pay for them over and over. Do yourself a favor and discard the item and the guilt.

Separate the items into three piles: keep, donate, discard. Keep the items you love and that you know you will wear. Put the items that you know you won't wear and that are in decent condition (i.e. someone else can still wear them because there are no visible holes, tears, or stains) in the donation pile. A note about donating these items: you can also try to sell these items online. Of course, that will take extra effort, but if you are up to the task, you may make some extra money! Items that should go in the discard pile are things someone else would not wear because the items are stained or ripped.

Remember to take baby steps. This process can be overwhelming. If you've worn items you are unsure of out of the house and are still unsure, put them somewhere you can't see them for a few months and put a reminder in your calendar. If you haven't missed the items in a few months, it's probably time to say goodbye.

Your Kitchen

Something people may not always think about when getting rid of unnecessary things is what is in their fridge. Take a look inside your fridge and ask yourself if you use everything that is in it. If not, why not? Has some of the stuff expired? Did you need it for one recipe you made last year and didn't like it? If so, it's time to toss whatever it is.

Apply the same process to your dishes. If there is anything broken, get rid of it. You should have gone through any duplicates during the duplicates exercise, but if you haven't, do that now. Look for duplicate cutlery or dish sets.

It's common for people to have many mugs. Again, this is a personalized process, so you get to decide just how many is enough, but it is a good opportunity to go through your mug collection and cull the ones that don't make the cut. Here are some questions to ask: Do I use it? Is it beautiful? Does it make me happy when I see it? Am I keeping it just because I am too lazy to throw it out?

Cookbooks are another item some people have many of. If you have cookbooks gathering dust because you tend to look recipes up online, it's probably time to donate or sell them.

Your Bathroom

You probably don't need to keep the three types of hair product you bought a few years ago that didn't work for your hair type. If you have a friend or family member that any of your unused products would work for and the products are still good, consider giving them a new home. Otherwise, if you are not using any of your toiletries it's time to say goodbye. The same goes for makeup.

This is also an opportunity to go through your small bathroom appliances. You can look for duplicates and check to see if any of them are broken. Let's face it, if you have two hair dryers you probably aren't using both of them!

Toys

If you have children or pets, you may want to go through their toys. This is another instance where you have to ask yourself what is being used on a regular basis. Get rid of anything that is broken and box or bag up what isn't being played with regularly and set it aside for a couple of months. If the things inside the box or bag aren't missed by the end of that time, it's time to donate them.

Your Garage

Your garage is a space that you should not expect to declutter all at once. If, like the junk drawer, your garage has become a dumping ground, this may take some time. The first step is to take an inventory of what you have, including in any boxes. Once again, look for anything that is broken and put those items in a discard pile. Look for duplicates. Is one of the things better quality than the other? Get rid of the lesser quality item. If you're unsure of any duplicates, put them in a box and out of sight for a couple of months. If you don't miss them, you can donate them. Like your wardrobe, your garage should reflect the lifestyle you lead now, not the one you led in the past.

Minimalism Challenges: It's Not Easy, but You Can Do It

As mentioned earlier, it is important to regularly do an inspection of your home for clutter that has managed to creep back into your life. Even if you are consuming thoughtfully, you are probably buying stuff. You may also have been gifted things that have now become clutter.

Once a month or once every couple of months, spend an hour going through your possessions and take an inventory. This includes your garage. Ask yourself again if you use the item, if you have more than one, and if you love it. If done with some regularity, you will find that this is a pretty quick process. Take your time with any new items that have found their way into your home. And always be honest about why you want to hold on to certain things.

The same goes for your wardrobe and accessories. During your regular inspections, you may find that certain items do not fit you like they used to, or that they don't suit your current style. You may also want to try the "one in, one out" rule when you buy a new item of clothing or accessory. This just means that for every new item you bring into your home, you donate or discard one.

This leads to another challenge with minimalism. It's the temptation to keep buying. We live in a consumer culture and we are constantly bombarded with ads for the latest and greatest thing that we just can't live without. Retailers try to lure us in by showing us how much better our lives would be if we just bought this one thing. They put up sale signs that make us wonder how we could possibly pass up such an amazing opportunity to own an item for such a low price.

This is where the list you created at the start of your journey will come in handy. Review your list on a regular basis to remember why you started in the first place. Regularly practicing gratitude for what you have will also help you realize that you don't need to buy more stuff.

One common challenge of minimalism is if you live with someone and they are not fully onboard the minimalism train. You may have disagreements about the things that you want to keep or give away and what things you may or may not want to buy going forward. If you find that your partner or roommate is in complete disagreement with your desire to go minimalist, start with your own stuff.

Going through your personal items will start you on your journey and will help keep the peace in your relationship. You can get rid of a lot of clutter even just by going through your own possessions. And who knows, once your roommate or partner sees the progress you've made, they may get on board!

Another suggestion for when you live with someone who is not into trying minimalism is to try and find common ground. Perhaps you can show them the clutter in certain areas of your home, be it a communal closet, a kitchen drawer, or a counter. Be patient as you go through the items with them and talk through why you should keep or discard each item. If you practice patience and continue to have the conversation without being pushy, they may start to come over to your side. Again, start small. Try decluttering one small area and live with it for a while. After a couple of weeks, ask what they think of the tidier space and if they want to try decluttering another.

Getting rid of gifts can be difficult. They may hold sentimental value, or you may feel guilt about the amount of money someone spent on the item. Or you might think the person who gave you the item will be upset if you get rid of it. The reality is that most people will not even notice if you get rid of their gift. They are too busy with their own lives. Of course, if you want to keep something because you use it or you feel it adds value to your life because it adds beauty to your home, then you should keep it. But don't hold on to something out of guilt or fear. If the person does notice and gets upset, explain why you got rid of the item. If they are a close friend or family member, they'll probably understand. And if they don't, it might be time to examine the relationship.

A note about getting rid of sentimental items: the memory is not attached to the actual item. It is inside of you. Keeping the item does not mean that the memory will stay fresher in your mind. Once you start clearing out old photos you no longer look at or trinkets that gather dust, you will be surprised at how little you miss them and how the memory associated with those items does not go away.

As with anything worth doing, there will be struggles as you embrace a minimalist lifestyle. But as you will soon realize, these struggles are far outweighed by the benefits.

Chapter 4: The Minimalism Movement

Minimalism isn't a new concept. People have been living simply and within their means for a very long time. For centuries, philosophers and religious leaders have touted a simple lifestyle as a way towards virtue, better knowing oneself, connecting with nature, and living as a unique individual.

On a more personal level, if you think about how your grandparents or great-grandparents lived, they probably led much simpler lifestyles than the majority of us today.

In 1845, author and philosopher Henry David Thoreau decided he would live alone in the eastern Massachusetts woods. His theory was that humans do not need much to be happy. Thoreau wrote his book *Walden*, which is based on his learnings while living in the woods. In *Walden*, Thoreau writes about self-reliance, living simply, and going against the status-quo (Huseby, 2019).

Since then, minimalism has cropped up multiple times in one form or another. In the 1990s, people participating in the *voluntary simplicity* movement were looking for a simpler life. They were tired of working long hours and wanted more meaning and purpose in their lives. They realized their possessions did not make them happy and wanted more time to do what they wanted to do.

How and Why Minimalism Has Become So Popular

If you Google the term minimalism, a slew of results pop up. For the last few years, it seems as though minimalism is everywhere. You can see it on Pinterest boards, on Instagram, YouTube, and the myriad of blogs out there. But there are good reasons why minimalism has become a movement.

The Great Recession started in late 2007 and many people lost their jobs and their homes. Because of the economy and the lack of jobs, people had to learn to live with less. Many embraced minimalism out of necessity.

In the years following the Great Recession as the economy started to grow, people did not forget what they or their family members went through. They wanted to remain self-sufficient because they knew that a recession could happen again. They also realized that living with too much excess was not making them happy.

Since then, minimalism has remained a strong lifestyle choice amongst many who do it for their own reasons. Below you will see some good reasons why minimalism has been steadily growing in popularity.

Environmentalism

With growing concerns over the environment, many people are turning to minimalism as a way to counter climate change. The production, transportation, and distribution of so many products is wreaking havoc on the environment. We're using up many resources faster than they can be replenished, and some resources sadly can't be replenished at all. Although on the individual scale it only has a small impact, becoming a minimalist and buying fewer things means using up less of the earth's resources.

Financial Reasons

Being in debt is a common incentive to become a minimalist. Credit card interest rates are incredibly high and buying unnecessary things that you don't need can wrack up a huge credit card bill. Living within your means, buying better, and buying less helps you save money.

Another financial reason minimalism has become so popular is the volatility of the global market. Many people suffered as a result of the Great Recession. Since then, we've seen rising unemployment and housing market crashes. We have also seen that wages don't always increase at the same rate as the cost of living. Uncertainty around jobs and the rising cost of everything from food to clothing means saving money now is more important than ever.

Freedom to Choose One's Lifestyle

Many people these days do not want to be tied to a 9 to 5 job. They have seen their parents and grandparents struggle through jobs that they did not enjoy, and they don't want that for themselves. Of course, if your 9 to 5 job makes you happy and is a good fit for you, that is excellent! But minimalism can create more choices if you decide to explore a different way of living. Wanting and having less stuff and less space for said stuff means you can save money. If you save enough, you might find that you need to work less.

Growing Consumerism

Consumerism has grown in recent years. Companies manufacture products that are never meant to be repaired and sometimes break down in one or two years. Products are deliberately made to be obsolete quickly so that consumers must rush out and buy the latest and greatest version. We are constantly told that we need things to make our lives better and to be a better person.

Consumers are tired of spending their hard-earned money on products they are told they need. Minimalism is a way of countering all of the noise from advertisements and the media. Once you realize that you actually don't need what advertisers tell you, you can be free of the constant noise pushing you to consume.

Increased Social Awareness

With social media and international news available to us anywhere and at all times, we can see how other people in the world live. And many people live with a lot less than we do. There is a huge discrepancy between the haves and the have-nots. We don't even need to watch the international news to see that many people are living in poverty or below the poverty line. There are people in your city right now living below the poverty line.

We now have a greater awareness of this discrepancy and many people don't want to contribute to it. Some people are becoming minimalists so that they have extra money to contribute towards charities.

As well, people are more aware now of the working conditions of garment workers in the fast fashion industry. Workers are exploited and taken advantage of. Many large clothing companies manufacture their clothing in places where people are very poor and have no choice but to work for whatever salary they can get. Proponents of the minimalism movement know that by buying better, more sustainable clothing, they are supporting workers in fair and equitable working conditions.

Authenticity and Self-Assurance

There is a growing movement of people who are seeking the freedom to just be themselves. Discarding the excess helps us discover who we really are, and what is truly important to us.

Something as simple as going through our closets and asking ourselves why we are holding on to certain items can make a big difference in how we see ourselves. It is the act of self-examination that will help us realize that we do not need a lot of possessions in order to let our true selves shine through.

Getting rid of excess possessions and knowing we can live without them is a huge confidence booster. People will understand what matters the most is not the sum of their possessions, but their values and the way they treat people. An authentic life is a happy life.

Developing a Personal Style

Minimalism is a way to stand out in a world with so many people trying to fit in. It offers us the chance to create our own unique personal style, whether that goes for decorating our house or choosing our wardrobe. Instead of trying to keep up with whatever the latest style or fad is, people who live the minimalist lifestyle focus on their own brand, whatever that looks like.

Less Choices to Make

Companies are manufacturing products at an almost alarming rate. The amount of choices we have when purchasing a product is staggering. Decision fatigue is real! Minimalism offers relief from that. By embracing minimalism, not only do we buy less, but we buy with intention. That means putting thought in our purchases and trying to purchase the best that we can afford. The parameters we put around our purchases, as a result of minimalism, can help us quickly narrow down the myriad of choices when we do need to buy something.

A Little Stability in an Unstable World

Minimalism allows us to be more self-sufficient. We get to decide what we consume and what we want to pay attention to. In an increasingly unstable and fickle world, minimalism allows us the opportunity to make our own choices. It helps us feel more in control of our lives and a little bit more stable.

A Little Peace and Quiet in a Complicated World

The modern world is complex. Technology makes us available 24/7, if we so choose. Minimalism allows us to examine what makes us happy and do away with the rest. It gives us space and time with our thoughts.

Technology

It's amazing what you can store on the memory of a tiny device these days. Our phones and computers can now store many of the things we may have been holding on to, like old photos, calendars, calculators, paper files, notebooks, phone books, and music. These little devices take up way less space and can be stored out of sight, if we choose.

Realizing That Things Don't Bring Happiness and Prioritizing Experiences Over Stuff

More people are realizing that material possessions don't make them any happier. With bigger credit limits now available to more people than ever, people have the opportunity to try out luxury items, even if they can't afford them. They are finding that their happiness level does not increase with the amount of stuff they own. People are increasingly asking themselves if going into debt is worth the amount of stuff they own.

Many people are starting to realize they value experiences over having things and would prefer to save and spend their money on a nice experience. They understand that stuff can only bring them happiness for so long, while experiences last in our memories a long time after they are done.

Aesthetic Reasons

The minimalist look has become more popular in the last few years because of its clean lines and simple designs. Minimalism pares an item down to its most essential nature, removes subjectivity, and aims for objectivity.

Easier Travel

We live in a global society and more people are traveling so they can experience different cultures. Many do it simply to relax during a two-week break from work. Whatever the reason, having less stuff to pack makes it easier to be mobile. Long gone are the days of lugging a giant suitcase behind you when you go abroad.

Improving One's Health

Many people choose minimalism as a way of taking control of their physical and mental health. They feel stress and anxiety over feeling like they have to keep up with others in terms of what success is. They stress over having the "right" clothes. They stress over being in debt. If their physical health is suffering, they often find they don't have the time to take care of themselves because they have commitments, like a 9 to 5 job.

Knowing that they do not have to spend all of their spare time cleaning and organizing their possessions helps people relax and stay calm. This is extremely important for mental health. Being able to sit in a calm environment rather than one full of clutter does wonders for a person's rest and relaxation.

By participating in a minimalist lifestyle, people find they have more time to practice habits that lead to better health. Having less stuff and owing less money means some people can choose to work less and instead focus on their health.

Self-Improvement

Many people are on a constant quest to improve themselves and to live a better life. Self-improvement has become a big goal for people in the past decade. Minimalism is a way to improve yourself and your life. After all, you need self-control in order to cull your possessions and to resist the temptation of consumerism!

Finally... People Want More Time and Life Is Short

As a society, people are realizing that life is very short, and time is very precious. People no longer want to be tied to their desk all day, every day. They don't want to work all of their lives and wait until they are in their 60s and 70s to fulfill their passions and travel dreams.

They want to have the time to do what they want, whether that's to pursue their passion or spend more time with family. Minimalism gives people more time. It does not necessarily guarantee that someone can quit their job, but it means spending less time on the care and maintenance of things.

As you can see, there are many reasons why minimalism has become so popular. And these are not trivial reasons. The world is changing, and minimalism is not going anywhere. We are constantly bombarded with advertisements and choices. The world can be overwhelming and stressful. Even though the concept of minimalism has been around for a long time, now more than ever it can help people find happiness, balance, and meaning in their lives.

Chapter 5: Minimalism and the FIRE Movement

As mentioned earlier, minimalism is a way to achieve financial independence. Needing less and therefore spending less means a person living a minimalist lifestyle can put more money in their bank account. And for many people, having more money in their bank account means more financial freedom to do what they want, including a possible early retirement.

The FIRE Movement

FIRE stands for Financial Independence, Retire Early. The idea behind FIRE is to save and invest at least 50-75% of one's income so one can retire early, in other words before the age of 65. The thinking behind this is if you can keep your expenses low, you can save more and thus reach financial independence earlier.

Financial independence can look differently to many people, but the biggest reason people seek financial independence is so that they don't have to have a full-time job, whatever that looks like for them. They can work part-time, if they wish, or not work at all.

Proponents of the FIRE movement are typically in their 20s to 40s and are looking to retire somewhere in their 30s or 40s. They decide on an amount of money that they think will allow them to live a comfortable retirement. Then they work and save between 50-75% of their income and once they have saved their predetermined amount of money, they either quit their full-time job or scale down to working part-time. Many people travel after they retire, and they do not work again. Some people work part-time during their travels. Others decide to go back to school to pursue a passion and start a completely different career.

There are some who focus on just one part of FIRE, be it financial independence or retire early. Some people are not interested in retiring early because they like their job and find it adds purpose to their lives. Some want to save for financial independence, but they are not willing to save up to 75% of their income.

Some FIRE proponents want to retire early, but it is so they can leave a job they dislike and follow their passion. Perhaps they want to go back to school to learn a new skill or they want to have enough money to quit their job and try their hand at a job that pays less money but is more fulfilling. And some people want to retire early so they can travel or sit on a beach.

One of the elements of the FIRE movement that its followers find very attractive is the amount of control they feel over their lives. People who strive for financial independence choose what they want to spend less on, whatever that looks like to them. It could be choosing to not go out for coffee every day, choosing to buy less clothing, choosing to not have cable, or choosing to cancel their internet. They also choose whether they want to move to a smaller home or to a less expensive area to save money. In a world where many people feel they do not have control over how they live their lives, this can be very attractive.

How Minimalism and the FIRE Movement Go Hand-in-Hand

Part of the FIRE movement is saving and investing a chunk of your earnings. Proponents of the FIRE movement do things like cutting their cable or internet, stop going out to restaurants, or stop getting takeout and buying new clothes. Many people feel like they have to deprive themselves in order to save the money to be financially independent, but it doesn't necessarily have to be that way.

Being a minimalist means you get to decide what adds value and meaning to your life. It changes the way you look at your possessions and makes you realize that you are more than your possessions.

Living as a minimalist can help you achieve financial independence without feeling like you are depriving yourself because you know what adds meaning to your life. You know that your time and freedom are more important to you than money. But it also means you get to decide what you cut from your life and what you keep. If you get depressed thinking about cutting your weekly coffee date with a friend out of your life, then you should keep it! The idea is you get to decide what you can part with, and the savings will follow.

Minimalism and the FIRE movement both go against the grain of what our society tells us is important. They teach us that we can have more control over our lives and that we get to decide what is important. Minimalism teaches us to rid ourselves of any excess. In turn, we start saving money because we are buying less and using less. We can save and invest that money and eventually, over time, we can become financially independent. With financial independence comes all sorts of freedom—the freedom to quit your job and work part-time, the freedom to quit your job and go back to school for something completely different, or the freedom to try a totally different career.

Both minimalism and the FIRE movement can be a little bit anti-establishment. Minimalists and proponents of the FIRE movement know they do not need possessions to make them happy, and they realize the American dream does not necessarily lead to satisfaction in life.

How Minimalism Can Help You Reach Your Financial Goals

Prioritize, Prioritize, Prioritize

One part of being a minimalist is reflecting on what is important to you and what things you can cut out of your life in order to be happier and to reach your goals. As part of this, being a minimalist means you can start to prioritize your spending. As you become more grateful for what you have, you will realize what few things are important enough for you to spend your hard-earned money on.

What is important to you? Try to think of the things you would spend your money on and make a list. If something is not that important but you would still like to have it or experience it once in a while, put it on the list but closer to the middle or the bottom. Perhaps it can go under an "Other" category. Obviously, things like mortgage, rent, utilities, and food would be at the top of the list. But what else would you include on that list? Writing down all the things that you need or want to spend your money on will help you become clearer about your spending priorities. It might also help to compare this list to the list of reasons why you want to be a minimalist.

Get Rid of Debt

Since you spend with intention and buy less when you are a minimalist, you can put the money you save towards paying down any debt you may have accumulated. Getting rid of debt is a big step towards becoming financially independent because it means you can start saving and investing more of your money. Perhaps you might want to consider adding debt to your priorities list, closer to the top.

Budget

Once you have your list of priorities, you can create a budget for yourself. Remember to apply the principles of minimalism here and keep it simple. Have a few categories in your budget, including an "Other" category for your non-essential activities or purchases. It is important to track your spending and compare your budget to your list of priorities. This way if you start spending more in the non-essential category, you'll know that you may need to revisit why you started your minimalist journey in the first place. Create a budget and stick with it!

Simplify Your Bank Accounts and Credit Cards

As emphasized throughout this book, minimalism is about trimming the excess. If you have five different bank accounts scattered across different banks and four different credit cards, maybe it is time to streamline. Most people need one checking account, so if you have more than that, look into why. Streamlining your bank accounts and credit cards is less confusing because it makes it easier to know where your money is and where it is going. Not having to keep track of all your different accounts means you can spend that brain power and energy elsewhere.

Set up Automatic Savings

Starting an automatic savings plan makes it easier to save money. It saves you time and you don't have to think about how much to contribute each month. It also helps you stick to your budget because you can factor in a specific amount you contribute towards your savings.

You can set up an automatic savings plan with your financial institution. Start small and see how it goes. If you find that you have more money to save, you can adjust your automatic deductions and your budget. After a couple of months of automatic deductions, you will be surprised at how much money you have managed to save. It is a simple step to take and your future self will thank you for it!

Set up Automatic Payments

Just as automatic savings makes it easier to save, setting up automatic payments makes it much easier to pay your bills once you have set up a budget. Automatic payments allow you to plan for the weeks that the payment will come out of your account and adjust your budget accordingly. It also helps you stick to your budget because you know that the money will be coming out of your account.

Buy Things Using Cash

Studies have found that we spend more when we pay using a credit card. This is because we have been bombarded with the mindset of "buy now, pay later." The trouble with that is we sometimes end up buying things that we can't afford because we do not need to pay up front.

Paying for things with cash helps you stick to your budget and makes it easier to keep track of where your money is going. It also keeps you away from very high credit card interest rates. When you pay for something using cash, you may find that you are more intentional with your spending. When you want to buy something and you take your cash out of your wallet, you may find you are less willing to part with it because you can physically see it.

You May End up Saving on Rent or a Mortgage

Once you lighten up on your possessions, you may find you don't need as much living space. You can consider moving to a smaller home and typically this leads to a smaller rent or mortgage.

Another thing minimalists often consider is moving to a less expensive area. If you determine that going out for dinner or coffee much of the time is not a priority and you would rather be closer to nature, perhaps you can consider getting a home outside of a major city center where things are typically less expensive.

Sell Unwanted Items

One small way to make money as you start your journey into minimalism is to sell your unwanted items. Once you have gone through your home, including your closet, and decide what you want to get rid of, you can choose to sell those items. There are many websites that will help you sell your unwanted items. Remember one person's junk is another person's treasure!

Conclusion

Minimalism is not just for single people with money and no kids. It does not mean you have to give up all of your possessions and live in a tiny home with no possessions. Nor does it mean you have to give up all of the things you enjoy doing. Minimalism should not make life harder for you because you are deprived of all the things that you like. You do not need to follow a stringent set of rules if you are interested in becoming a minimalist. Finally, minimalism does not just apply to your possessions.

Minimalism is a tool. It is a tool that can help you determine what you want to get out of life and how to get there. It is a way of living intentionally so that you are not robotically going through the motions of life but are living authentically and being true to yourself.

Minimalism is about intentionally getting rid of the excess in your life. People choose a minimalist lifestyle for many reasons. They want to minimize because they are stressed, have health issues, are in debt, want to spend more time with family and friends, want to be financially independent, or they simply want to have more energy.

Prioritizing is a major theme in minimalism. When you are starting on your minimalism journey, it is important to prioritize what is important to you in life. Ask yourself how you want to spend your time and who you want to spend it with. Create a list with all of the reasons you want to live as a minimalist. This list will come in handy when you find yourself tempted to spend money on something you are not sure that you need.

Prioritizing your spending is an important way to figure out where your money is going and what you would like to do with it. Prioritizing your spending will help you to create a budget and to stick with it. And in turn, that will help you save more money.

Being intentional is an important part of minimalism and some might say it is the central theme to minimalism. You must be intentional about what you want from your life, what you choose to keep, and what you choose to get rid of. You should also be intentional with your spending because this will help you save money. If you are not thinking about what you are spending your money on, you will not be able to keep track of it or the things that come into your home!

When you do go out to spend your money, be sure to consider quality over quantity. Don't be tempted by the sale signs! Look for things that will last a long time and that can be repaired. Not only does that mean you get to keep the item for longer, but it means you get to keep that thing out of the landfill for longer. Another great thing about quality items is that they are usually timeless so you will be happier with them and less likely to think about replacements.

When people think about minimalism, many think about their possessions. Being a minimalist means living with intention in all areas of your life, including your health, your commitments, your relationships, and your finances. Think about getting rid of what doesn't serve you in the different areas of your life.

Your time is precious and finite—don't spend it with people who don't appreciate you and who you can't be yourself around. Your health is also precious. If your diet is full of all sorts of processed, unhealthy foods, think about why you consume that type of food and what you could eat instead that would be better for your health.

Minimalism has become more popular over the years and for many good reasons. Growing concerns over our environment make the principles of minimalism very attractive. After all, more people buying less stuff means using less of the earth's precious resources to produce, transport, and store all of the products we consume. It also means less excess that ends up in landfills.

A minimalist lifestyle can also lead to financial independence and an early retirement. People are realizing life is too short to be stuck in a job they dislike. Even if they like their jobs, people want more freedom to do the things they want to do. Minimalism can help you achieve your financial goals. By prioritizing your spending and making a budget, you can start saving towards being more financially independent. That means you can pay off your debt, go back to school, reduce your hours to part-time, or quit your job altogether.

Finally, minimalism is about freedom. The freedom to choose to live life your way. You decide if you want to listen to advertisements about the latest fads. You can choose if you want to be part of the consumerist machine—to work 40 hours a week, or more, in order to pay for things you don't need, with money you don't have. Or you can choose to spend your time in a way that serves you, a way that lets you follow what your soul and heart desire.

It does not take a lot to start on your journey towards minimalism. By following the ideas set out in Chapter 3, you will be well on your way. Remember that you determine the time you want to take on your journey and the excess that you want to trim. Following someone else's course can lead to frustration. It is important that you do this for your own reasons and on your own timeline.

There is a better way to live. It is a less stressful way of living and a gentle way of living. It helps you live the way you want and not how society, the advertising industry, or big business wants you to live because it affects their bottom line. There is a better way and it's called minimalism.

References

12 Struggles of minimalist beginners and how to overcome them. (n.d.). Nomader How Far. Retrieved January 12, 2021, from https://nomaderhowfar.com/blogarchive/12-struggles-of-minimalist-beginners-and-how-to-overcome-them

A brief history of minimalism: How the minimalist movement happened. (2019, July 21). Minimalism. https://minimalism.co/articles/history-of-minimalism

Becker, J. (2010, May 28). *10 Reasons why minimalism is growing.* Becoming Minimalist. https://www.becomingminimalist.com/10-reasons-why-minimalism-is-growing-a-k-a-10-reasons-you-should-adopt-the-lifestyle/

Becker, J. (n.d.). *When you're a minimalist but your partner isn't.* Www.Becomingminimalist.com. Retrieved January 12, 2021, from https://www.becomingminimalist.com/when-youre-a-minimalist-but-your-partner-isnt/

guest. (n.d.). *Minimalism on the path to Financial Independence (FI).* Www.Becomingminimalist.com. Retrieved January 12, 2021, from https://www.becomingminimalist.com/financial-independence/

How to become a minimalist (or just simplify your life a little). (2019, January 2). Be More with Less. https://bemorewithless.com/how-to-become-a-minimalist/

Huseby, M. B. (2019, October 2). *Life at Walden Pond: Thoreau's lessons on minimalism*. Medium. https://medium.com/swlh/life-at-walden-pond-thoreaus-lessons-on-minimalism-2a16388efd44

Krier, J. (2020, January 1). *The 10 Principles of Minimalism*. Minimalist Focus. https://minimalistfocus.com/the-10-principles-of-minimalism/

Long-term effects of chronic stress on body and mind. (2016, May 1). Psych Central. https://psychcentral.com/lib/long-term-effects-of-chronic-stress-on-body-and-mind#4

Maiti, R. (2020, January 29). *Fast Fashion: Its detrimental effect on the environment*. Earth.org - Past | Present | Future. https://earth.org/fast-fashions-detrimental-effect-on-the-environment/

McFall-Johnsen, M. (2019, October 21). *How fast fashion hurts the planet through pollution and waste*. Business Insider. https://www.businessinsider.com/fast-fashion-environmental-impact-pollution-emissions-waste-water-2019-10

Move For Hunger, The Environmental Impact of Food Waste. (2015, May 11). *The environmental impact of food waste | Move For Hunger*. Moveforhunger.org; Move For Hunger. https://moveforhunger.org/the-environmental-impact-of-food-waste

Rebecca. (2020, January 27). *The rise of the minimalist movement*. Minimalism Made Simple. https://www.minimalismmadesimple.com/home/the-minimalist-movement/

Start here. (n.d.). The Minimalists. https://www.theminimalists.com/start/

What is the F.I.R.E. Movement? (n.d.). Daveramsey.com. https://www.daveramsey.com/blog/what-is-the-fire-movement

What is ultra-processed food? (2018). Heart and Stroke Foundation of Canada. https://www.heartandstroke.ca/articles/what-is-ultra-processed-food

Lightning Source UK Ltd.
Milton Keynes UK
UKHW021835301222
414659UK00005B/192